ONLINE BUSINESS IDEAS

20 Tips Of How To Use Social Media To Get Your Business To The Next Level In 2 Weeks

MARK AUSTIN

© **Copyright 2016 by Mark Austin- All rights reserved.**

The follow eBook is reproduced below with the goal of providing information that is as accurate and reliable as possible. Regardless, purchasing this eBook can be seen as consent to the fact that both the publisher and the author of this book are in no way experts on the topics discussed within and that any recommendations or suggestions that are made herein are for entertainment purposes only. Professionals should be consulted as needed prior to undertaking any of the action endorsed herein.

This declaration is deemed fair and valid by both the American Bar Association and the Committee of Publishers Association and is legally binding throughout the United States.

Furthermore, the transmission, duplication or reproduction of any of the following work including specific information will be considered an illegal act irrespective of if it is done electronically or in print. This extends to creating a secondary or tertiary copy of the work or a recorded copy and is only allowed with express written consent from the Publisher. All additional right reserved.

The information in the following pages is broadly considered to be a truthful and accurate account of facts and as such any inattention, use or misuse of the information in question by the reader will render any resulting actions solely under their purview. There are no scenarios in which the publisher or the original author of this work can be in any fashion deemed liable for any hardship or damages that may befall them after undertaking information described herein.

Additionally, the information in the following pages is intended only for informational purposes and should thus be thought of as universal. As befitting its nature, it is presented without assurance regarding its prolonged validity or interim quality. Trademarks that are mentioned are done without written consent and can in no way be considered an endorsement from the trademark holder.

Table Of Contents

Introduction 1

CHAPTER 1 Social Media Platforms And Demographics 2

CHAPTER 2 Facebook 9

CHAPTER 3 Twitter 16

CHAPTER 4 Linkedin 21

CHAPTER 5 Market Social Media Through Brick And Mortar 27

Conclusion 30

Introduction

Congratulations on purchasing this book and thank you for doing so.

The following chapters will discuss ways to increase traffic to your business utilizing several social media streams.

There are plenty of books on this subject on the market, thanks again for choosing this one! Every effort was made to ensure it is full of as much useful information as possible, please enjoy!

CHAPTER 1

Social Media Platforms And Demographics

Marketing a business is a constantly changing full time job. Before the internet, promoting a business was limited to paper and television ads, and there really wasn't much to it. The goal was to find your target market, determine which newspapers and magazines they read, and place your advertisement. It was easy to find out if it was working. Your customers would come directly to your business. You could count them, and ask where they heard about you.

Today's market is much different. With the inception of the internet and online shopping, the marketplace has changed. Most of the old tactics no longer work. Even worse, the internet is flooded with information, so your ad creativity must be on point to be noticeable in a sea of other advertisements. Not to mention that people have learned to disregard pop ups and other ads, making the need for more creative marketing solutions. The internet created a heavy flow of information that adapts and changes quickly. For advertising to be effective now, marketing needs to be prompt and relevant at any given moment.

The good news is, billions of people worldwide use social media sites like Facebook and Twitter to keep up with friends and family, news stories and current events. This makes media sites like these a free and easy way to promote your business. Unfortunately, this is not a new concept, and most businesses are already doing this, flooding the marketplace with ads. Your job as a savvy business person is to cut through all of the other ads to promote your company that is both effective and enjoyable for your followers. After all social media is supposed to be fun and exciting. Your ads must be as well.

If you are new to social media, your first job is to explore your platform options. Take a look around to see what social media sites people in your target demographic are using. This is crucial so you don't waste time trying to appeal to people outside your demographic. Just as you wouldn't post an ad for life insurance in a teen magazine, you wouldn't use certain sites that cater to demographics out of your reach. It isn't worth the time and effort.

First off, you should definitely be on Facebook. An estimated 75% of the population is on Facebook, and most of those people visiting the site on a daily, if not hourly basis. Instagram and Twitter come in close second and third. Don't forget about Pinterest and LinkedIn as well. There are an infinite number of other sites that you may find helpful, however the reach isn't as broad, and may be specific to your field. For example, platforms like Snap Chat, a place to post pictures and short video clips the moment they happen, may be appropriate for a food blogger or travel expert, but would likely not work for an accounting firm.

Here is a quick rundown of what each big site offers their patrons:

Facebook-This platform allows you to connect with old friends, colleagues and family. Members can post pictures, videos and tell their "friends" about things they are doing on their timeline. They can "tag" certain people in photos to identify them. Friends can then "Like", "Share" or "Comment" on the post to show interest. Any time someone reacts to a post, it is reposted on their own timeline, which gets shared with all of their friends.

A post can easily be shared between numerous people, connected in real life or not, in a matter of hours. When this happens, it is called a "viral post", one in which millions of people have access to. In recent years, businesses were allowed to create pages as well, allowing for spectacular marketing opportunities. Many businesses use Facebook as a primary advertising source, utilizing the momentum of organic sharing to get the word out about their business.

As far as demographics are concerned, it is a safe bet. About 75% of the population is on Facebook, and usage among age group, gender and income is relatively even. Everybody uses it. If you are new to social media, this site is a good place to start. It is relatively user friendly, and it will only take a couple of days to get used to its functions. They also provide lots of options with businesses in mind, making marketing much easier.

Twitter-This platform is similar to Facebook, but allows users to speak their mind in 140 characters or less. It allows only a snippet of text to keep things simple, making people sum up their lives or experiences in short detail. Links can be added other sites as well. One of the best features of Twitter is the hash tag (#). While this concept is now a popular tool on all social media sites, Twitter was the first to introduce it. Members can create new hash tags, for example, #eBook.

Any time a specific hash tag is used in a post anywhere online, it is linked to the hash tag. You can then search a hash tag, and all of the linked posts will show up in one place. This is genius marketing, especially for events and popular trends. You will often see specific hash tags created for weddings, so as guests post pictures, they can be linked together, making an impromptu wedding album online. Hash tags are not exclusive, and can be used by anyone, anywhere.

Users are typically younger adults in urban areas, so this platform may not be appropriate for all business types.

Instagram-similar to Twitter, this site allows members to post photos and videos to their circle of followers. Instagram also utilizes hash tags to build viewers and create viral videos. Instagram is different because the app includes filters that are used to modify pictures and videos. Endless filters are available and can change colors, retouch photos, add funny pictures, captions and more.

Users are primarily younger adults of non-white descent. While this may not be the most practical social media sites for a full blown campaign for some businesses, it can certainly be utilized in combination with other platforms to promote your business. Since this site is really demographic specific, it may not be the most fruitful social media platform for your business, but giving it a shot could get you connected with a market you have yet to reach. Never underestimate the power of reaching a new audience.

Pinterest- Lots of people use Pinterest to find recipes and ideas for DIY home projects, however it can be used to search for ideas for just about any topic. Members can "Pin" links to website onto their profile, then can go back to them later. It is essentially an online bulletin board for things you find interesting. Members can organize their profile by creating "boards" to pin things from different areas of interest. For example, you could have a recipe board, a craft project board, and ideas for Halloween costumes. The possibilities are endless.

ONLINE BUSINESS IDEAS

This is a social page because you can follow people or businesses and get updates on things they post to Pinterest. For example, if you really like recipes posted by a certain business, following them on Pinterest will give you access to new things as they are posted. Pinterest can also be used to promote blog articles or your website. In your publications, give your readers the option to "Pin" the article or parts of articles. This gives your article more exposure, since it then becomes part of the Pinterest network. It can be shared by just about everybody. You will also see more pingbacks to your site because the person that pinned it will likely be traveling back to your site to take a second look. Any way you can get additional visits to your site means you are getting positive engagement, which is the key to business growth.

Women under 50 living in suburban areas are the biggest Pinterest users. Just like Instagram, this platform may not be a winner for every business, but it is worth a shot. Race and income level does not play an important role in user status. It also does not take as much effort to maintain a Pinterest page. Your business could simply Pin an article once a week and duplicate its presence on Facebook and Twitter. It takes little effort. If this platform proves to be a big winner for your specific situation, paid ads can be built to expand your reach even more.

LinkedIn- this site is mainly used as a way for business professionals and colleagues to stay in touch. Members can create profiles that show their current jobs, past work and education experience and much more. Clubs and professional associations create pages to join as well. This site mimics a professional networking event online. You can get in touch with former colleagues and new people who are in similar lines of work. Discussion forums about topics of the trade are common, and it pays off to be a member of groups in your field. Discuss ways to promote your business, what has worked for other people, and create business relationships. Hiring managers have a tendency to hire from pools of people they are already in touch with. This can be a great way to find a job, or at least a new opportunity for your business.

Usage is popular with working-age people and post collegiate with high income levels in urban areas. Businesses catering to job recruitment or business solutions should definitely consider membership with LinkedIn, although any working professional will find some sort of benefit from joining.

YouTube- Videos are the main focus of this platform. Individuals and businesses are allowed to post videos about any topic. You will see just about everything. From funny cat videos to workout routines and makeup tutorials, YouTube has it all. Get directions on how to fix a car or complete a home improvement project. As a business, YouTube gives you the opportunity to post videos about subjects in your field. For example, accountants can give a tutorial on how to save money, or a gym can give workout tips. Give the viewers something useful, and then shamelessly plug your business at the end. It's a win win. Cross post your videos on other social media sites to draw more attention to them.

Demographics vary widely depending on subject matter of the video. Because YouTube is so broad, you are best off determining how much competition you will have with your subject matter. For example, there are millions of people looking up cosmetic products on YouTube, but there are also millions of makeup tutorial videos. Your chances of getting a good following are slim. However, if you are one of a select few businesses with a very specific product, your reach could be better. If you decide to start producing videos, try to find topics that are trending, and provide content that hasn't already been done. This can be a difficult task, so dig deep and find obscure topics in your field that people may find interesting.

Should you develop a large following, it could become another income stream. Advertisers pay to post ads on heavily trafficked pages. Profits go to you, the video supplier.

Now that you are familiar with some of the most popular social media platforms, it is time to pick which ones you want to use. Utilize the demographics information at the end of each description to pick two or three platforms you want to use. Remember that you will need to make time to maintain each site on a regular basis in order to build a following. If you are new to social media, start with one platform, Facebook, and concentrate on that until you are comfortable.

In the following chapters, you will find tips and tricks to use with different social media platforms to increase your online presence, and in turn, increase sales and foot traffic to your business.

CHAPTER 2

Facebook

Facebook is one of the most-used social media platforms out there right now. Over 100 billion people worldwide are on it. It is no secret that it will pay off to use Facebook, a free platform as part of your marketing strategy. Here are some tips to use Facebook to your advantage.

1. Engaging posts

Even with its amazing social outreach, Facebook is becoming a tired spot for advertising. Newsfeeds are constantly bombarded by ads, both clever and subtle, or obvious and obnoxious. If you have ever scrolled straight past something that was a blatant ad, most likely, your followers will as well if you post something that is very obviously an ad. Post things that are relevant both in time, place and to your target market. Make sure not to just post sales flyers and reasons to buy your product, but also things that people find interesting about your field in general.

Post questions and comments about hot topics in your field and ask your followers to give their opinion. For example, if you are in the field of nutrition, don't continually post ads about the services you offer. They already get it. While a few blatant offerings of service are important, focus your content on relevant subjects, like a new research article proving that eggs are really okay for cholesterol. Experts say to keep your true advertising posts to one in every seven posts to maintain a good following.

Go ahead and link the source of an interesting article in a post, but remember to write a little something about it, preferably, something posing a question. For example, with the egg article, provide the link and ask something like, "Who's excited that we can eat eggs again?" The point is to be engaging and human, something your followers will relate to.

Remember that humans are simple creatures, and we like pictures. No matter how interesting your text is, if it's not accompanied by a tantalizing picture, most people will just scroll past. Find something colorful, creative and relevant to the message you want to post. Avoid clipart style photos that are a dime a dozen. You are better off posting a picture of your business in real life that people will recognize.

2. Link back to your website or blog

Don't assume that people who follow you on Facebook know that you have a website, or that you painstakingly write blog articles every week. Let them know. Most blog and website platforms allow you to automatically post updates to social media sites like Facebook. This allows a link to go straight to your Facebook page every time you publish work, without any added effort. That's great for a busy professional like you.

Don't forget that the opposite is also true. Make sure to post links to Facebook on the title page of your blog, and in every post. Set it up so people can automatically share your blog post to social media sites like Facebook, Twitter and Pinterest. Options exist to print and email your articles to friends and family as well. Remember that most people will not bother to share something if it involves more than a couple of clicks, no matter how good your article is. Make it simple and easy for people to share and they will reward you with more clicks.

3. Create a call to action-coupon or offer

Facebook has added lots of options that make marketing easier for businesses. Try creating an offer or event that is relevant to your business. Under create an offer you can create an online coupon good for a dollar amount or percentage off the customers next purchase either online or in store. You can set expiration dates, terms, and conditions, just like a real coupon. All of your followers will see it, and if they choose to redeem it, will receive periodic reminders about the offer until they have used it, which is essentially more free advertising.

A great tactic is to create an offer that provides you a benefit, besides that of another sale. For example, ask your customers to write a review on Facebook in exchange for a percentage off their next purchase. Not only will you get positive (hopefully) on your Facebook page that draws more followers, you will get the sale on top of it.

Remember to tell your current patrons that there are added benefits and discounts available exclusively to Facebook followers. Create flyers and posters showing the benefits of following your Facebook page and other social media accounts. Yes, they are already your customer, but their friends and family may not be. Their Facebook friends will begin to see the posts your current customers like, and your reach will grow.

Create an event for open houses, one-day special sales, classes and more. Events are great because they post more than just as a story in your follower's timeline. It creates an event reminder in that person's calendar that must be addressed. Followers can respond by accepting or declining your event invite, but either way, it is customer engagement. Should they choose not to respond, Facebook will send automatic reminder messages prompting them to respond.

4. Use page insights

Facebook has a clever little tab that will show you your page stats. See each individual post and how well it performed. You will find stats on how many people the post reached, and how many people liked and engaged in the post. You will also find stats on how your page did through time, compared to itself.

The page has a list of each of your posts, how many likes and how many shares it received. What you want to pay attention to most is the organic reach. When you think of organic, think of a plant growing. The plant must have a seed to get it growing. This is your post. Once the seed is in the ground (Facebook) it begins to grow when it has enough light and water. Those are your likes and shares. The more light and water, the bigger the plant is able to grow. On Facebook, more likes and shares leads to a bigger following, similar to the blooming plant.

Organic reach is a great indicator of interest because it shows how many people were interested in the post, and how well the post traveled just by organic measures of liking and sharing. A high organic reach shows that your followers liked the post, and then their friends liked the post, and so on. Use this information to develop future posts that could also grab the same attention.

Also watch what areas of your business do best. For example, if you own a sporting goods store and you start to notice that posts about hiking and camping do better than tennis or basketball, adjust your posting strategy. Give your followers what they want and post more information about camping gear. Use this information to coordinate sales and other brick and mortar marketing strategies. What is popular may change over time, especially in a seasonal market like sporting goods. Different activities are popular depending on the weather, so just like your sales, adjust to the upcoming trends with your posts.

It is also okay to ask your followers what they want. Yes, you can rely on your stats and page likes, but sometimes it is a good idea to just come out and ask. For example, let's continue with the sporting goods theme. If a new product comes out that is not part of your current inventory, take a poll to find out if people would be interested in buying. Promote the product showing its benefits and see how people respond. In your post, literally tell people you are considering carrying the product, and tell them you are trying to gauge interest. Remember that most people relate better to a business that has a true human element, and most try to support local businesses when possible. Big box businesses have focus groups to tell them what products to carry. Small, local businesses have their target audience, so utilize it. Show them that you care about their opinion, and they will notice.

Another cool feature in Facebook Insights is "Pages to Watch". Here you can select pages that are similar to yours and Facebook will keep tabs on their stats against yours. This is useful in a number of ways. First, and most obvious, you can tell if a competing business has a better following than you.

Second, it allows you to see their post engagement for the week. Once you begin watching a page, look for sudden spikes and dips in their engagement, then compare what has been posted on their site that may have caused it. This is beneficial, especially if your page has become stagnant. Find out what topic made their engagement skyrocket, and provide your audience something similar as it is trending. For example, celebrity watching is a pretty volatile business. If you don't have a scoop on a new story, your viewership will likely decrease.

Watch other pages for spikes in engagement for a clue of what is trending. You may not have the scoop on the story, but most likely your viewers would react if you were to ride the coattails of your competitors and post something a little late.

4. Boost posts

Just like any good business, Facebook has options to pay for advertising. You can create advertising, like a virtual flyer, that will post to people outside of your current following. Also choose to boost a post that did well on its own. Boosting means that you are paying to reach potential customers you don't already have. With your posts, you are limited to the number of people who are currently following your site. You are also at the mercy of those followers who will only pass the word along to their friends and family if they like your post. Still, the likelihood that your post will go viral and touch a whole group of untapped potential customers is slim.

When you boost a post, you can tell Facebook what type of demographic you are looking to reach and in what geographic area, then they set up a list of new people to send it to. The benefit here is that you will be reaching new people, rather than everyone who already knows about your business. This expanded reach can really improve your following, and as following increases, so does foot traffic in your business. The only downfall is that a boosted post shows up as a "Suggested Post" on a person's newsfeed. Most followers say that they often skip over these suggested posts because they have not been posted by a friend. They recognize that it is an ad, and are less likely to click on it to avoid annoying pop ups. However, if you can create content that is engaging enough to get past this barrier, you will do just fine. It is still worth a shot.

That being said, do your research first. Now that you are fluent with Facebook Insights, use it to create content that will already have a great organic reach, and then pay to boost it and reach a new group of people. Say a particular post that reviewed a new product did very well. People were engaged, interested and willing to buy. Choose to boost that post and reach a whole new audience. Test this on a small market before you spend a large amount of money. Watch the paid reach on your insights page and compare it to organic reach. If your paid reach increases your organic reach exponentially, you will know that this was a good investment. If not, experiment with a few different kinds of posts to really understand why boosting did not work.

An offshoot of boosting posts is promoting your local business. You will find this under the "Local" tab on your insights page. Here you will see how many people are in your local area and what demographic age group they are in. You can send out a local promo to Facebook followers in a close radius to your business for more exposure. Pay attention to the demographic though. For example, if your local demographic of Facebook followers is young people under 30, you may not find it helpful to advertise your fundraiser for the senior center. While there are caring people under 30, this is not your target audience.

It may not be appropriate to boost posts or locally promote all the time, if at all. If your organic reach is already growing your business exponentially, don't bother boosting posts. If you feel your following growth has slowed, try boosting a post to jumpstart traffic again. Just watch your insights instead of blindly spending your marketing budget. Know your market and best times to promote, just as you would for in-store ads and newspaper marketing.

CHAPTER 3

Twitter

1. Customize your Twitter page to mirror your brand

Your logo is your biggest branding source, so put it out there whenever possible. On Twitter, any time you tweet something, your logo pops up. This is free branding for you, and the more you post, the more familiar people will become with your brand.

This works especially well for businesses with brick and mortar stores, or with products in big box stores. Your logo and color scheme will become instantly recognizable among a sea of other product choices. Your Twitter handle just may put you at the head of the pack!

It is also possible to customize your page with colors and media that are part of your branding. Use your brand colors as background and insert pictures where possible. Don't forget to fill out your business bio, as this is your chance to market your services to potential customers. Never leave it to chance that your followers know about everything that you have to offer.

2. Create a list of followers

This process is really about taking your networking skills online. Just as you would seek out people with similar interests at an in-person networking event, do so on your Twitter page as well. Follow businesses and high-profile people that share common interests, and that are relevant to your business. For example, if you are in the field of graphic design, follow your favorite magazines and local or national designers that are doing excellent work.

As you follow people, they will begin to notice that you are following them, and they will then follow you. Include current customers and acquaintances that are likely to use your services.

Don't forget to include competitors. They likely have their eye on you, make sure you are up to speed with their latest and greatest ideas as well. Remember that direct competitors can become customers and business partners. Never use Twitter, or any social media page to slam your competition.

3. Address tweets to specific businesses, publications, high-profile contacts

Twitter is all about networking. After you create your page, be sure to seek out similar businesses to follow. Once followed, you will begin to see their Tweets in your news feed. This is a good way to keep up with sales and trends in your field. Use this information to formulate some posts of your own. Just as you can follow a business or specific person, they can follow you too. Your reach broadens when followers of someone you are following begin to see your posts too. These people may not have been a part of your original circle, but they are now. Get this going by following someone, then making regular comments on their tweets. They will begin to notice you, and follow you too. Let's say you own a gym. If you follow a local nutritionist, go ahead and comment on

ONLINE BUSINESS IDEAS

their posts about exercise. Ask questions. Engage with them. They will engage with you in return, creating the relationships that you need to grow your business.

Depending on your type of business, positive praise for an accomplishment is best, yet respectful criticism can spark your followers as well. Just remain tasteful and professional. Your social media is a reflection of your character and your business, and a tasteless comment will quickly shut your following down.

4. Create a landing page

Utilize Twitter's option to create a landing page. This page will mimic the home page on your website, giving business information like the physical address and phone number. Give a brief yet concise description of your business, how you help the community, and appeal to your target audience. Give a quick rundown of what people can expect of your Twitter page.

Explain what topics you plan to post about and people that you like to follow. If there is a benefit to following you on Twitter, like helpful insider tips or Twitter-only coupons, let them know. Think of this page as advertising to recruit new followers. Most people take a look at this page before following someone. Include links to your website or other blog sites that correspond to your business.

5. Respond to direct mentions and messages

Remember that most potential customers appreciate local businesses with an engaged owner and staff. If someone sends you a compliment or question on Twitter, show that you are paying attention and respond! This will win people over by showing that you play an active part in your business, and that you care about your followers, customers and their opinions.

To keep people interested, pose questions that engage your followers to respond and ask follow up questions. If you plan to do this, make sure to check your account regularly so you can respond to questions in a timely manner. The internet age has spoiled us with an influx of information. If you don't answer someone's question quickly, all they need to do is use a search engine to get their answer. Don't give business away.

Treat negative feedback very carefully. If you get a dismal review on social media, reject your urge to respond swiftly, and probably in the wrong way. Never respond solely based on emotion. Take a step back and really read through the review to make sure you can understand the problem. For example, if you own a restaurant, you will likely receive a bad review here and there from a disgruntled customer. They may say the food was bad or the service was horrible. Don't go on the defensive. You can't please everybody.

Remain diplomatic and respond with respect. You could say, "We are sorry you didn't have a great experience at our restaurant. We would like the opportunity to make it up to you. Here is a coupon for a free meal on us." While you may not be able to win over every customer, you can at least show them, and the rest of your followers, that you are dedicated to their satisfaction. Had you responded emotionally and said that they simply don't appreciate good food, you are likely to lose them as a customer permanently. Also, people are more likely to talk about a bad experience than a good one. You bet that unsatisfied customer will tell their friends.

6. Follow trends and use them to your advantage

Take a look at the sidebar of your Facebook page. It will show you things that are trending at that particular moment. Keep an eye on this frequently and watch for trends that are related to your business. Write posts and blog articles about things that are trending in a timely manner. Make sure to post something as quickly as possible because trends come and go very quickly. That means you shouldn't take a week to write a blog article about something that is trending, as the trend will likely have passed by the time you write the article. If you feel like a topic that is trending is very appropriate to your business, take advantage and post something small. For example, say that the Whole 30 diet is trending on Facebook, and you have a business in nutrition and wellness. If you don't have time to write a full article with your blog, consider making a Facebook post with a short opinion piece on the diet. Make it short and concise, but leave your followers wanting more. Have them contact you for more information should they want it. This is a good way to get your phone ringing.

Check trending hash tags and use them when appropriate.

CHAPTER 4

Linkedin

LinkedIn is a great platform to add to your arsenal. This site is different because it is primarily used by professionals looking to connect with other professionals, unlike Facebook or Twitter which are more for recreational use. Using this site gets you in touch with a whole different audience. It is a great resource for all business types, but especially for those in businesses that thrive on helping the success of other small businesses. For example, an accountant or marketing company will be able to obtain new clients through LinkedIn pretty easily, while a business like a nutritionist or therapist may only get lucky if an individual is interested for their personal health.

Either way, it is still a good thing to connect with people that are in similar lines of work, as you likely have the same customer base. As an example, a nutritionist may not get new customer accounts directly, but after creating a relationship with local gyms and doctors offices, new referrals may get to them indirectly. LinkedIn also has forums so that like-minded professionals can share ideas and business strategies, which could be crucial to the development of your business. Not only can you connect with professionals, if you are hiring you can look for good candidates for positions and post ads for your open positions. Since LinkedIn members are usually those with an already developed skill set, most likely you will find some high quality candidates.

The key to making LinkedIn work for you is to get all of the details right.

1. Create a profile that won't be ignored.

Making your profile is a chance to get all of your work, volunteer and personal experience out there. A LinkedIn profile is different from those of other social media. It is essentially an online resume that anyone on the site can look at. While you may not be looking for a job, it is still a good idea to showcase your skills to others in your field. You never know when you could get a new opportunity or business venture.

Start with the basics of your current position. Here is a good place to showcase the ins and outs of your current business. Explain your job title, especially as owner, all of your day to day tasks and overall goals of business. Also showcase your past experience. Most business owners have worked in other fields in the past, so go ahead and let people know how those skills will translate to your current field. For example, an auto body shop owner that has experience with general repairs and upholstery could pick up more work simply if people know all of the other things they are capable of. Don't forget to add media like pictures and videos to each job description entry. If you worked in marketing, showcase your work visually and show people what you did. Pictures often speak louder than words. While you are at it, add a current professional profile picture. Remember that this is a professional site, so the picture should be one you would put on a business card or your website. No vacation pictures! People like to see who you are, and could help you recognize colleagues at physical networking events and conferences.

Utilize LinkedIn skill tags. Under skills and endorsements, pick some key words that sum up your skills. If you are in healthcare, pick tags related to your skills, like "nutrition education", "diabetes", "patient care". These show up on your profile, and your connections can also go in and endorse you for your skills. This basically shows that others in the field can vouch for your experience, giving you more credibility.

2. Make connections with like-minded professionals.

This is all about how you play the game. Do your research and find local businesses in the area that probably have a similar market to yours. For example, an accountant may want to network with a payroll company or human resources firm in the area. All of these businesses could cater to other businesses in the area, making their desired demographic the same. They will be able to share ideas on how they recruit new customers. Ideally, they could refer customers between businesses if a good working relationship is established. This is a win-win for all parties involved because they are not direct competitors. Each runs a separate business with different functions, therefore, nobody loses at the success of another.

3. Make connections with direct competitors

It may seem counterproductive to make friends with direct competitors in your geographic area, for the most part, the opposite is true. If you can build a trusting relationship between your business, and a similar one just up the street, good things can happen. Let's say two ice cream shops open up within 5 miles of each other. There will be obvious competition between the two, however, the market share is good enough to support both businesses. These two shops could work together in a strategic way. To start, each business should have a signature dish that is special to their business. It would not be a good business strategy to do the same as everyone else in the area, regardless of relationships with local competitors.

Let's say Business A is set up to hold birthday parties for kids, while Business B is able to do custom ice cream cakes for weddings and other parties. If Business A is asked to make a wedding cake that they are not capable of doing, they would likely need to turn them away. A nice solution would be to refer them to Business B for their needs. In return, Business B can refer large parties to Business A in the future. Everyone benefits when there is mutual respect and trust between competitors.

There will always be situations where one party may take advantage of the other, and that is an inevitable downfall of business. Be careful to monitor your relationship and make sure that the trade is even. If you feel that your competitor is taking advantage of you, keep the secrets of your business close at hand. On the other hand, if you feel your competitor is making a good effort to refer customers to you, make sure you do your part to return the favor.

4. Actively participate in professional forums

Joining a professional group keeps you up to date with everything new in the field. You will be in the know on the latest and greatest research and products, which keeps you ahead of the curve. Here you can share positive experiences and ask questions when you have problems. It seems this works very well with most business types, but benefits service industries the most. Practicing doctors and therapists have a tough job of an ever-changing client base. Each patient is different, and must be handled on a case-by-case basis.

For example, say a doctor has recently seen a patient with a rare medical condition. All of their training and experience has not prepared them for this particular case. Forums give the doctor the opportunity to converse with others who may have the experience they are lacking, answering questions that will benefit their patient.

Being an active member of a forum gives you the opportunity to share your expertise with others. If your advice is good and well respected in the community, you will find these people coming back to you in the future. The doctor that gave their colleague advice on the rare medical condition may find other colleagues coming to them for advice, or simply referring patients that they feel they can't handle.

5. Consider Business Plus features

LinkedIn is a free site, but like any good online business, they offer additional services for a fee. LinkedIn Premium has options for individuals who are job searching, and specifically for businesses. Here, you can connect with professionals who might not be in your normal circle of contacts, expanding your network. It also lets you chat with those people, something you cannot do with the free service. Introduce yourself and let them know how your business can work from them.

Advanced services also let you see who has viewed your profile. The free service lets you see the last 5, but advanced is unlimited. Regular checks can show you how far your reach is, and how those people found you. It is a good way to measure the reach of your entire marketing plan, through all social media sites and your website.

Most importantly, advanced LinkedIn accounts offer online tutorials and classes to further skills in your field. Brush up on old unused skills, or learn something new that could improve your business. Learn how to use technology to streamline your business, accounting and management skills and much more. As

ONLINE BUSINESS IDEAS

a business owner, you know that you are never done learning, and this is a simple way to keep expanding your knowledge.

CHAPTER 5

Market Social Media Through Brick And Mortar

Just as people online would not have found your brick and mortar without advertising online, so it is the other way around. Let your regular brick and mortar customers know you are available on social media. With the majority of the population on at least one social media site, your efforts will be well rewarded. When they follow you, their friends and family will begin to recognize and follow you too.

1. Use social media logos on in-house paperwork

Brick and mortar companies tend to have lots of paperwork to hand out. Professional services like therapists and accountants tend to give out folders and cards to their patients and clients. Just as you would use a logo or letterhead on anything that leaves your business, use social media logos as well. The great thing about social media is that most websites are well established, and their brand recognition is so strong that a simple logo, devoid of their name is still recognizable. For example, we all know that a blue "F" symbolizes Facebook, and a light blue bird means "Twitter". Add them to headers or footers to let people know you are online. If you have space, give a quick explanation of what you typically post on social media. For example, a company focused on health and wellness could use the Pinterest logo, and a simple statement saying "visit this page for healthy recipes".

Try boosting your social media following by creating an offer to your in-house customers. Make flyers or coupon cards to hand out with the social media information. A great offer to try is to give a percentage off of a purchase for liking the Facebook page, or following you on Twitter. People often respond positively and do what you ask them to do if they have some sort of incentive.

2. Add social media tags to email correspondence

Use your email for more than business correspondence. Use it as an extension of social media. Add social media icons to the bottom of all emails to customers, colleagues and suppliers. You never know where your next customer will come from. Get more of your current contacts to follow you on social media by letting them know you are members of their favorite sites. Adding these icons can easily add time to your daily to do list, so make it simple for yourself. Most email platforms, like Microsoft Outlook allow you to store a signature block. Normally, this will be your name and title, address, phone number and other contact information. Add your website address and social media icons to cover all of your bases. Think about the last email you received from your favorite business. Their email probably had all of those things, and so should yours. Enter all of this information as a saved block and quickly add it to all of your correspondence.

If you don't have an email platform with this option, simply create one in a Word document and copy and paste it into your emails. Just don't forget to make active hyperlinks so that interested people can simply click on the icon to get to your site. If the link doesn't work, you will likely be losing about half of interested followers.

3. Create a bank of customer reviews

This works especially well with Facebook. Have customers review your business through Facebook so that new visitors will see all of the positives about your business. People are heavily swayed by the opinions of others. Let them see those good reviews!

Simply ask your best patrons to do a review for you. Most people would be happy to promote a business that they frequent. If you are unsure, prepare to offer an incentive for a review. Try offering coupons for discounted goods and services in exchange for their review.

4. Create a marketing strategy specifically for social media

Most likely, you have a marketing strategy and budget that helps you keep up with newspaper ads and dates for sales. Do the same with social media management. Create a plan that will be a template for your posts. Plan to post at least once a week on each individual social media site. Just like your marketing plan, do frequent evaluations to determine what sites are working best for your marketing efforts. Experiment with posting more and less on each site to determine where your time is best spent. The good news is, most features on social media are free, so it doesn't hurt your bottom line to experiment with different options.

Conclusion

Thank for making it through to the end of this book, let's hope it was informative and able to provide you with all of the tools you need to achieve your goals whatever they may be.

The next step is to set up a new social media marketing plan. Remember to build a plan that is easy and maintainable. Make sure you have time to give the necessary attention to each social media site you participate in. Utilize some or all of these tips to boost your following quickly.

www.ingramcontent.com/pod-product-compliance
Lightning Source LLC
Chambersburg PA
CBHW061236180526
45170CB00003B/1319